The Wellness Journal

Sharon Kinder

Illustrations by: Ivy Trazsi – LeMoon Illustration.

Medical Disclaimer

The information contained in this book is provided for education. It is not intended as, and should not be relied upon as, medical advice. The author is not responsible for any specific health needs that may require medical supervision. If you have any underlying health problems or have any doubts about the advice contained in this book, you should contact a qualified medical, dietary, mental health practitioner, or any other appropriate professional.

NB: All recommended links were correct at the time of going to press.

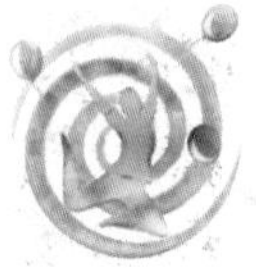
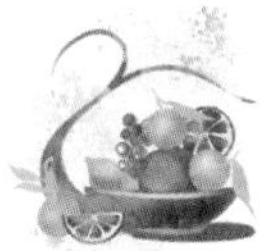
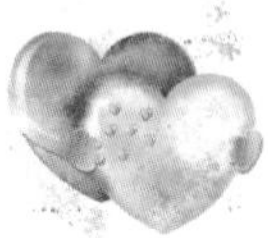
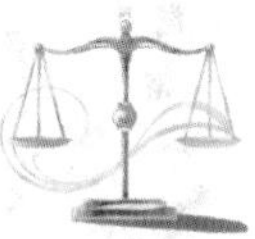
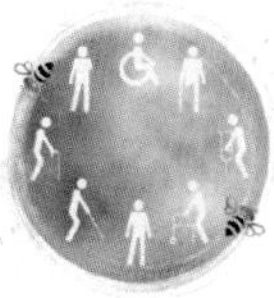
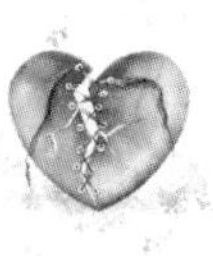
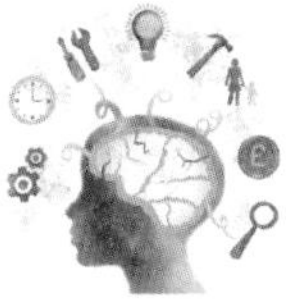
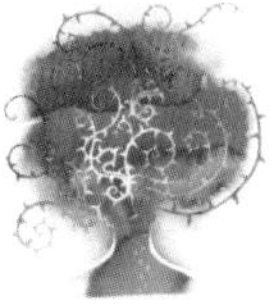
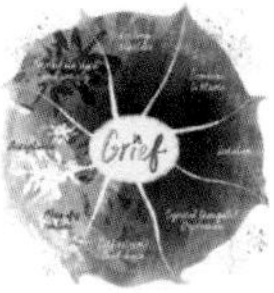
Grief
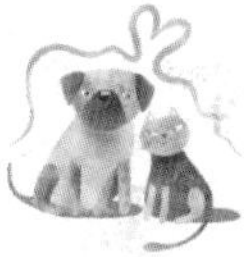
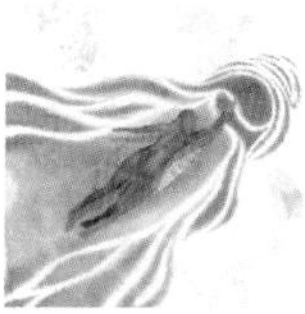
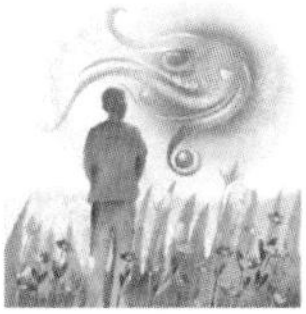
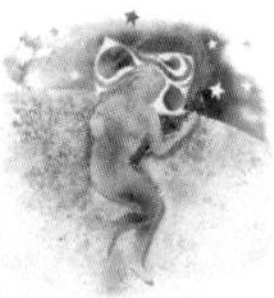

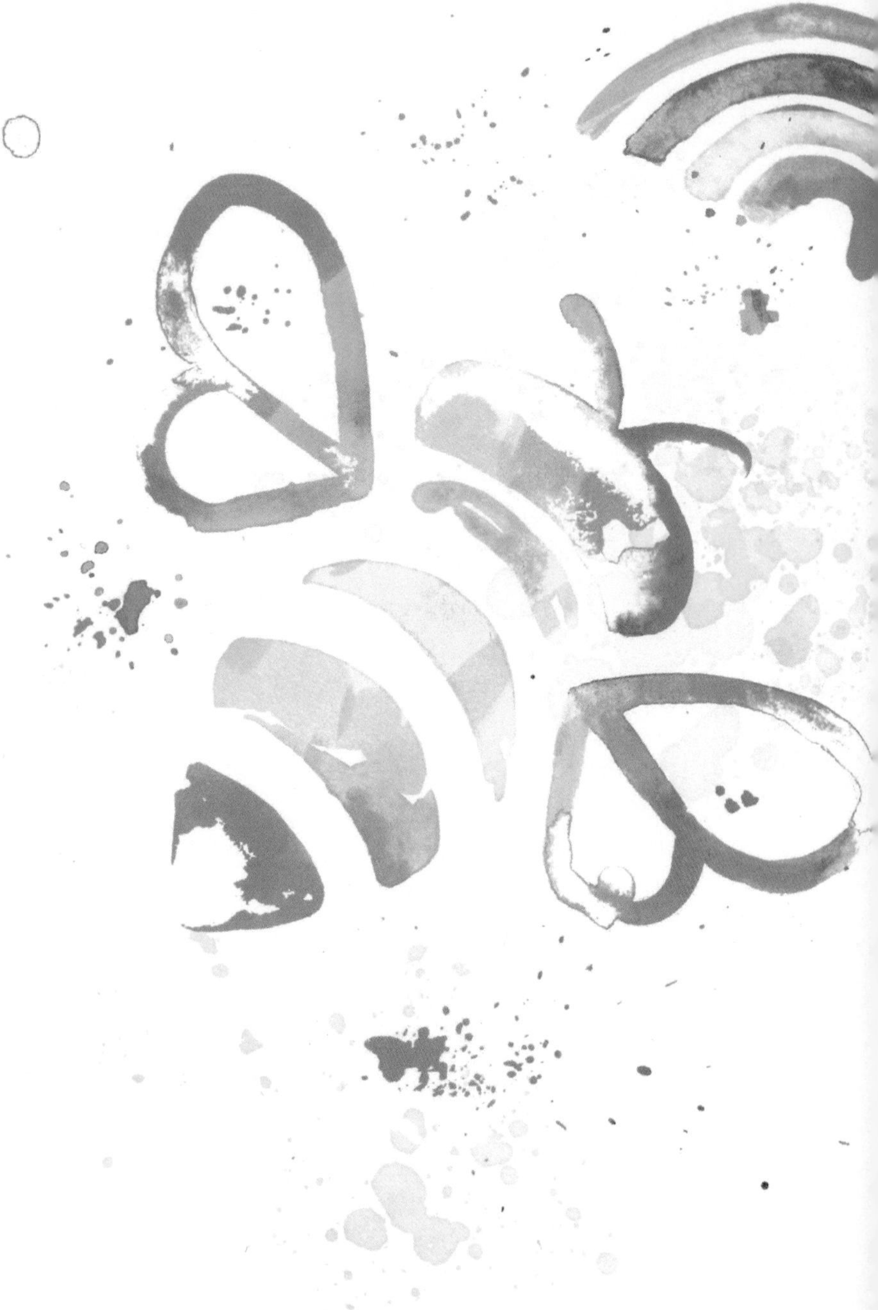

Why I Wrote This Journal

I hope you enjoy this journal and that it will provide you with support and comfort. We all have mental health; some days are fantastic, and we feel on top of the world. Some days can be harder than others. When we are growing through things, and our worlds go into turmoil, we don't always realise its effects on our health. Recognising those behaviours and making tweaks, talking, or seeking further support can help us on a speedier road to recovery. I wrote this journal from my own experiences to help and support people.

What Is in This Journal

In this journal, I talk about wellbeing, and the impact of the curve balls and blind bends life throws at us. Understanding ourselves and our behaviours will give us the insight to do something about it. It won't make these challenges go away but having a 'better you' may give you more resilience to make changes.

Remember, we are all a work in progress.

How to Use This Journal

The journal has been designed in a way for you to read, reflect and think about yourself. Become more self-aware and make notes.

About the author

Sharon Kinder (Pegg) has worked as a professional in HR for over 25 years, specialising in 'Inclusion' and 'Wellbeing'.

Sharon is a Fellow at CIPD, coach, mediator and trainer in both Adult and Youth MHFA and has developed relationships with a number of corporate clients both internationally and here in the UK.

Sharon's centre of the universe is Huddersfield, where she was born and bred and still lives with her son Sam and two Labradoodles.

Mental Health has been Sharon's passion and focus for several years. Sharon engages with people from all walks of life (and herself) to understand the impact mental health has on every single one of us; the good, the hard, the brilliant, and the difficult.

Contents

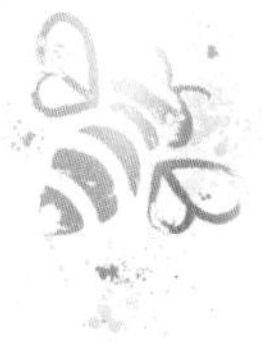

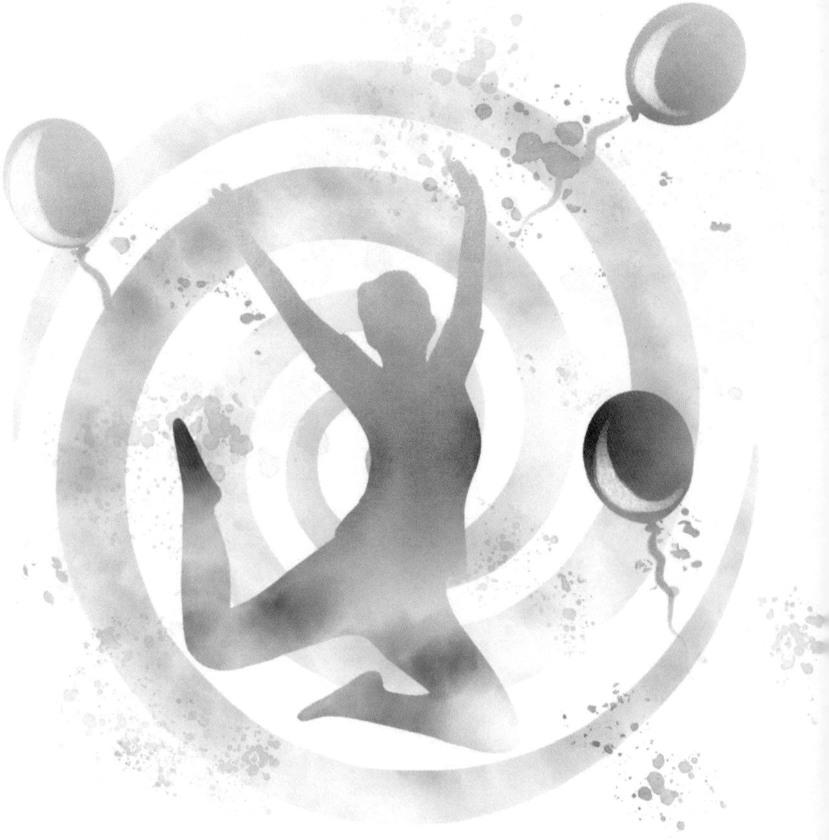

1

Wellbeing

What is wellbeing?

'Health is a state of complete physical, mental and social wellbeing and not merely the absence of disease or infirmity.'

An important implication of this definition is that mental health is more than just the absence of mental disorders or disabilities. World Health Organisation (WHO).

Wellbeing to me is when I feel both physically and mentally strong, a feeling of contentment, joy, happiness, and peace. We will all have our own variation of what that means to us.

The way I was brought up, we never discussed wellbeing, mental health or other words associated with our emotions. I was always told 'just to get on with it', 'there is always someone worse than you', 'tomorrow is another day', 'what have you got to be sad about?' I wholeheartedly believe that the messenger always had the best intent and desire to make me feel good about myself.

We know that we don't learn about this stuff at school – and yes, I am using the word *stuff* because that is what it is called. This stuff comes at us from nowhere, the stuff that we deal with all the time, the stuff that sometimes makes us feel consumed. So much so that, at times, we don't even stop and look at the *stuff* and the impact that it's having.

Pressing pause on a busy life is a gift we can all have.

To understand how we can look after our wellbeing, I am going to ask you a number of very important questions.

At the end of each section, you will have a chance to reflect on what those questions mean to you.

Reflection: What is wellbeing to you? Do you put yourself at the top or the bottom of your busy days?

Reflection Notes

_____

_____

_____

_____

_____

_____

_____

_____

_____

_____

_____

_____

_____

_____

_____

Exercise One - The Stress Container

Stress containers are a brilliant way of being able to understand yourself. The stress container can visually help us to understand our own vulnerability – it can also help us to be thankful for all the good stuff in our worlds. Take a moment to reflect and think about all the things that are causing you to 'stress'. Empty your head by writing them in the box.

Stress Box 1

Write down all your 'Stressors' in the space below then go to Box 1.	Examples
	• Caring for Parents
	• Children
	• Work
	• Relationships
	• Illness

Write yours in the space below ...

1.
2.
3.
4.

Coping Strategies Box 2

Write down all your coping strategies below and then go to Box 2	Examples
	• 20-minute walk
	• Talking to friends
	• Gym
	• Reading books

Write yours in the space below ...

1.
2.
3.
4.

Unhelpful Coping Strategies Box 3

Can you identify any? Write down any you can think are relevant and then go to Box 3	Examples
	• Drinking more than usual?
	• Pushing yourself excessively
	• Bottling up feelings

Write yours in the space below ...

1.
2.
3.
4.

Box 1

Ask yourself some questions:

How do I feel about each of the stressors? What is the impact on me?

Is there anything I can change?

Can I get any help or support?

Which do I need to prioritise first?

Am I worrying about things that are out of my control?

NB: These questions will give you some focus and help you to create a plan.

Box 2

These are all the things you enjoy doing that give you some time off from all those 'stressors' of the day.

What are your 'go to' strategies?

How much time do you get to give yourself a break?

What stops you from doing this?

Extra Thoughts

What can I change?

Box 3

At times, when we are under pressure, we do not always identify with or acknowledge our unhelpful coping strategies.

Identifying what these are can help us seek help, support, or even manage things differently.

What have you learned by listing your unhelpful coping strategies?

I personally do this exercise regularly and it gives me clarity on what is taking place. I do find that when it is written down it can look different. It helps me to see things with less 'fog'. It also helps me to understand more about my behaviours and feelings and when my body starts to react.

Notes

Notes

Notes

_____

_____

_____

_____

_____

_____

_____

_____

_____

_____

_____

_____

_____

_____

_____

_____

_____

Notes

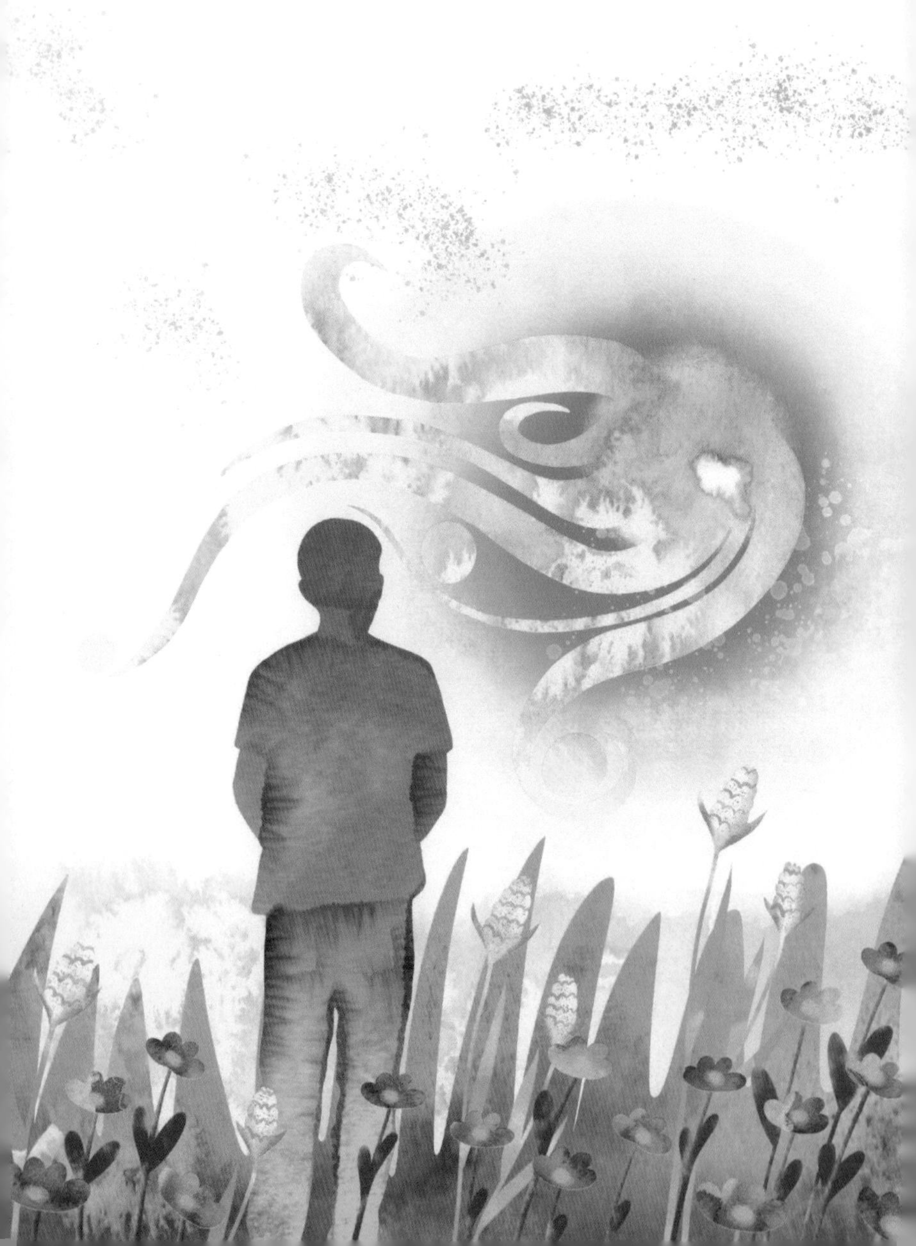

2

Reflection

What is Reflection?

'Life is truly a reflection of what we allow ourselves to see and be.'

When everything is going your way, and you feel on top of the world, how do you feel, and I mean truly feel?

What does your body do naturally?

When I consider this question, I think about how I feel lighter; my face is relaxed and has a natural smile. I somehow feel taller (and I need that at 5ft), shoulders back, being more aware of what is going on, and in short, I just feel damn good!

Vs.

When I am low, I can find it hard to concentrate; my shoulders ache, almost like an invisible cloak that can get heavier and heavier. I need the invisible cloak to tell the world I am fine – and I will be honest, I have a closet full of them for every occasion. My sleep pattern goes to pot; my mind feels constantly busy – with, yes, just stuff. And all the things I know I should do – and don't! Mainly because I am on the treadmill of life, and I am powering through.

What I have realised is that life is also about pressing the pause button to check in on me, to make sure I am ok, being self-aware and noticing my giveaway signs. We all have them.

How do we talk to ourselves to do those check-ins? What are those little voices saying to you, or do you not listen? Of course, language is a curious thing – and sometimes we don't always have the language to empathise and understand what we or another is feeling - good or bad! But let's be honest – it's much easier to talk about the good. But how do we talk about those feelings when this starts to change?

Nobody has a magic wand to make things disappear, but acknowledgement, changing it up, understanding why you are feeling the way you are and creating a plan to keep you on track can all help (we will talk about life's anchors later).

Reflection: How well do you know yourself? What is your good v. bad?

I want you to think of a moment when you feel under pressure. It might be when you are taking an exam, attending a job interview, or speaking in public.

What does your body start to do in those anxious moments? Write them down below.

1..

2..

3..

4..

Did you know our bodies can give over 100 different signs when under pressure? Not all at the same time, but your bodies have a unique way of communicating. It might be for some dry mouth, sleep challenges, brain fog, sweaty palms or cannot keep still.

Now think about when everything is going your way, and you are in a really good place. Now, what is your body doing? You are possibly walking with your head held high and shoulders back. Decision-making may seem easy. Your face is probably more relaxed, and you may even notice that you are sleeping better than how you normally sleep.

What does your body start to do in those positive moments? Write them down below.

1..

2..

3..

4..

How does each list compare?

..

..

..

..

Challenge: *Keep a log of your behaviours each day to understand the changes in you, both good v. bad.*

Understand and know yourself – if these are becoming persistent behaviours, do you know why? Is there anything keeping you awake at night? What else is going on in your world?

Notes

Notes

Notes

Notes

3

Self-
Importance

Why am I important?

'Self-care is how you take your power back.'
Lalah Delia

You are important because there is only one of you.

Do you like what you see in the mirror?

I ask this question time and time again, and the number of people who say 'no' is astounding. For many of us, we do not see ourselves as being important. We are comfortable with our 'job' titles - mum, dad, auntie, brother, manager, director, etc. They help to provide us with an identity and maybe even a purpose. But we can almost act into those roles. When we go through those challenging times in our life, we forget who we are, how important we are, and our feelings, goals, and personality traits. We can get lost and consumed with all this 'STUFF'!

Let's look at some of the stuff coming at us – the plates we are spinning!

News, parents, caring responsibilities, bills, jobs, family, relationships, homes, kids, grief - we are keeping these plates from falling off and spinning them like mad. Most of the time, we can do this with ease, but when other 'STUFF', sometimes the unexpected stuff (I call these blind bends), can take us by surprise, we often run at 110mph to keep it all in the air. We are not stopping for fuel or that intake of oxygen because we are a machine. We just keep going.

However, we know this can be consuming. We are simply trying our hardest to keep it all together.

At this point, are we putting ourselves top, middle, or bottom? Possibly the latter...if we are being honest.

Somebody once told me this great analogy!

When we board an aircraft, the aircrew is seating us and asking us to pay attention to the safety demo - by the way - they know a chunk of us have switched off already, possible thinking about the destination point and what we are doing when we land.

The part where they say – *and when the oxygen masks drop, you will secure them on yourself first!* The aircrew knows who will and who won't. But that aircrew is dead clever; they know that we cannot survive without oxygen. But every day in life, how often do we give someone else our oxygen first and forget about our own needs.

What happens if we get to that oxygen tank and it is empty? What happens to all that 'STUFF' in our worlds?

Reflection: Selfcare is important – you need around one hour a day, giving you time out from all that 'STUFF'. You need to put yourself first in order to carry on and manage the stuff – the good and the bad.

We are all very special, unique people. We are all accountable to ourselves; start giving yourself the best version of you.

Talk to friends
Watch TV
Read books
Gym
My pets
Hopi/massage
Reflexology
Gratitude

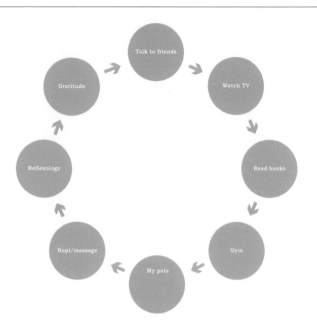

This is my 'wheel of self-care' – these are some examples of things that I do daily/weekly/monthly to give myself some timeout. I do 60 mins every day, including a mixture of things that help give me 'me' time.

What does your 'wheel of self-care' look like?

Fill in the blank circles on the page opposite and identify how much self-care you spend on yourself. Please also ask yourself the following questions.

1. *Do I spend enough time on myself?*
2. *How can I break down that 60 mins into chunks that can work for me?*
3. *How much variation do I have between the self-care categories?*

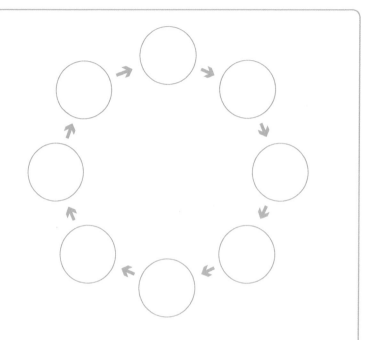

Recommendation: Self-care strategies should also be reviewed to ensure they still give you what you need. We all go through changes; sometimes, we might need to mix it up and try new things. If you are trying new things, before you rule them out, try them four times and then assess if it's for you or not. Sometimes some of the things can take time to gel!

Notes

Notes

Notes

Notes

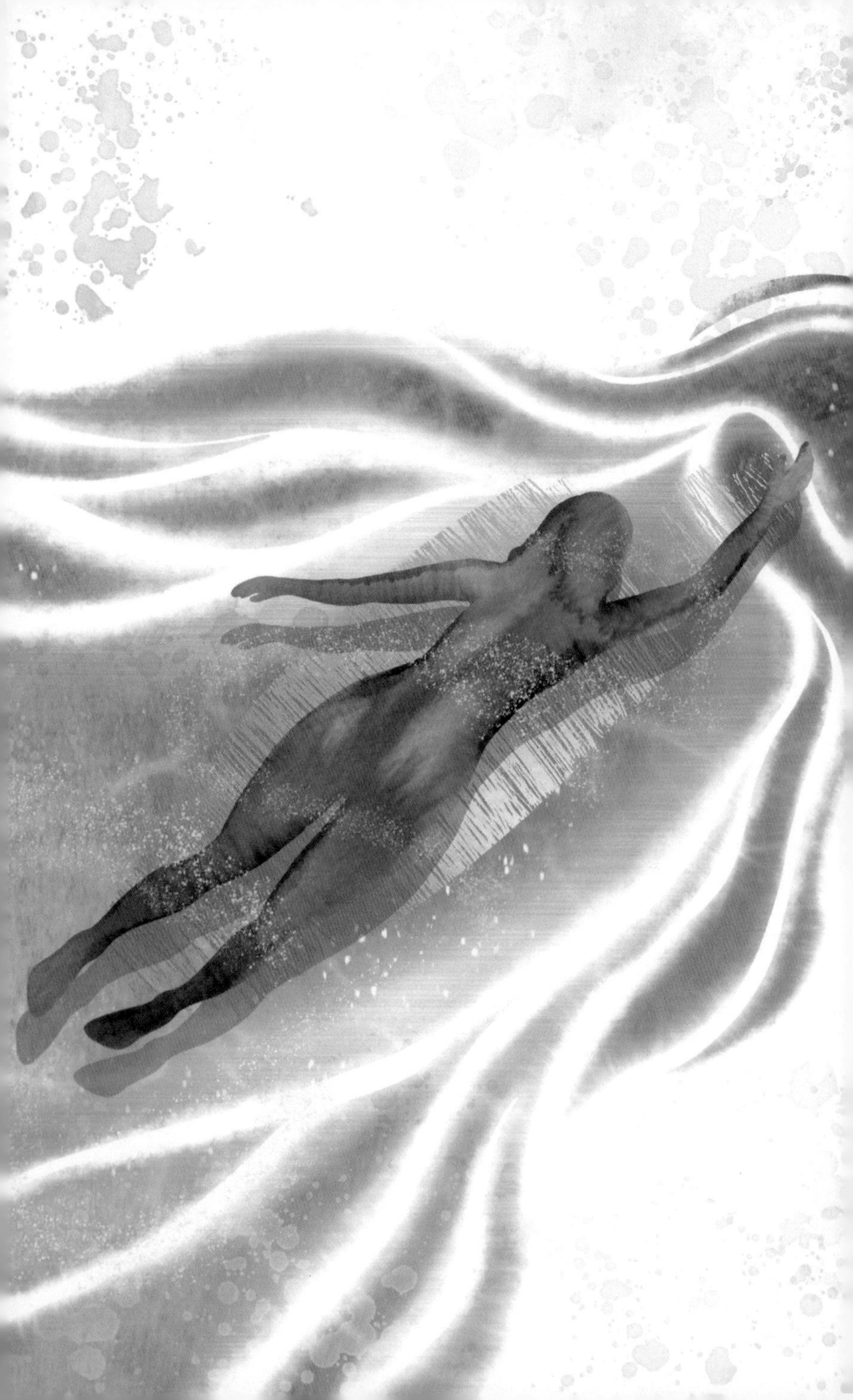

4

Self-Confidence

What is my self-confidence?

'The most beautiful thing you can wear is confidence.'

Your self-confidence is a belief in yourself. It is your capacity to make decisions and believe they are the right ones. It is a trust in your own judgement. It is also about accepting who you are, even those little imperfections—silencing those voices in your head. You know, the one that tells you that you can't do it.

We gain self-confidence in a number of ways, for example, through our experiences, our achievements, and the people who believe in us. We know that when we have self-confidence, it can have a waterfall effect on other people by inspiring confidence in them. For example, when we believe in ourselves, we talk with authority, our tone of voice changes, we can exude positivity, and we inspire people around us.

Compare this to somebody in your world who lacks confidence. How do they present themselves? Now think about your self-confidence. Does it change in a different situation? Do you believe in yourself?

Sometimes we can lose self-confidence for a number of reasons. We know that when our mental health is low, this can impact our self-confidence. For example, it might be a change in a situation, being bullied or even grief. We certainly know that when it oozes, it can be like a sieve, and we cannot stop the flow.

We can also be our own worst enemy and set impossible huge goals – we all have the ability to rubbish ourselves when we make a mistake or don't achieve the highest of standards. Yet we also forget to congratulate ourselves when things go well – this may go back to our frame of reference and how to behave in situations as children. Don't whoop too loud or yell; contain your excitement – that fear of being judged in a different or negative light. When we gain more experience, this type of fear factor may lessen, and we may realise that 'those' people's judgements and critiques are less important.

Self-sacrifice is another area that can impact on our self-esteem when our needs are not being met. Some people may not even know what their needs are, but something feels like it's missing. This can cause conflict in relationships.

Reflection: How many times do you put others before your own needs?

Reflection Notes

_____

_____

_____

_____

_____

_____

_____

_____

_____

_____

Let's take a look at your self-care in more detail.

Write next to each day how you have considered your own self-care needs. Write against each day what you have done for your own self-care and the time you have taken. The aim is 1 hour each day.

Example:
Sunday: Walking for 30 mins, meditation for 10 mins, speaking to a friend for 20 mins. 1 hour watching my favourite TV programme.

Monday: Yoga 40 mins, reading book 20 mins.

Tuesday: etc...

Wednesday:

Thursday:

Friday:

Saturday:

There are four pages to follow to carry out this activity over a 4-week period. Do you notice a pattern? Where can you make tweaks to priorities yourself?

Week One

Monday: _____

_____

Tuesday: _____

_____

Wednesday: _____

_____

Thursday: _____

_____

Friday: _____

_____

Saturday: _____

_____

Sunday: _____

_____

Week Two

Monday: _____

_____

Tuesday: _____

_____

Wednesday: _____

_____

Thursday: _____

_____

Friday: _____

_____

Saturday: _____

_____

Sunday: _____

_____

Week Three

Monday: _____

_____

Tuesday: _____

_____

Wednesday: _____

_____

Thursday: _____

_____

Friday: _____

_____

Saturday: _____

_____

Sunday: _____

_____

Week Four

Monday: _____

_____

Tuesday: _____

_____

Wednesday: _____

_____

Thursday: _____

_____

Friday: _____

_____

Saturday: _____

_____

Sunday: _____

_____

Notes

Notes

_____

_____

_____

_____

_____

_____

_____

_____

_____

_____

_____

_____

_____

_____

_____

_____

Notes

5

Self-Esteem

What is Self-Esteem?

'I am a measure of my worth, and I say I am worthy.'

Self-esteem is one of the basic human motivations in Abraham Maslow's hierarchy of needs. Maslow would suggest that individuals need both esteem from other people as well as inner self-respect. These needs must be fulfilled for an individual to grow and thrive. We need both to thrive and grow. Self-esteem is learned behaviour. It is not something we were born with, and we can all work on building our self-esteem – here are some ideas.

Many things can help build our self-esteem, family, friends, colleagues, supportive workplace culture, and acquaintances. Another thing to consider is how we can identify when our behaviours are changing - notice yourself. Be your authentic self, set goals and list your achievements. Congratulate yourself when things are going well and enjoy the moment.

Reflection: Think about somebody you know who has good self-esteem. What do you notice about them? Think about their body language as they walk into a room, their voice, how they look, and how they hold their head high. Write down what you 'like' about them.

Activity:

From the reflection, write down three goals based on the 'likes' you listed about that person. Think about how these can enhance your self-esteem. This is not about being a clone of someone else, these are things that will support you on your journey.

Date:
Goal 1.

Goal 2.

Goal 3.

Reassess these goals in 3 months to see how you feel then.

Date:
Goal 1 – Feeling

Goal 2 – Feeling

Goal 3 – Feeling

If you are ready for your next set of goals copy and repeat.

Notes

Notes

Notes

Notes

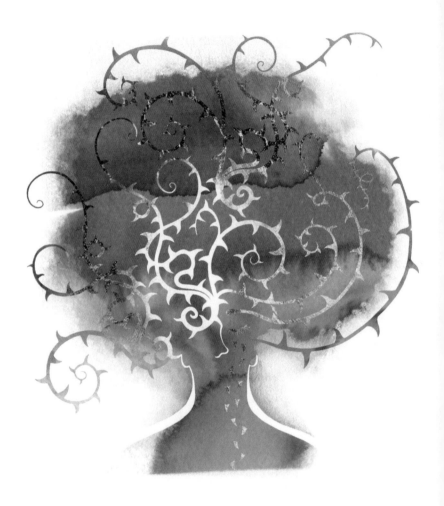

6
Resilience

What is my resilience?

'I can be changed by what happens to me. But I refuse to be reduced by it.'
Maya Angelou

Your resilience is successfully adapting to changing, challenging and difficult life experiences. Good resilience means we are coping emotionally and mentally with flexibility in our approach to those adjustments. Our resilience levels can change depending on our experience or what is happening in our lives.

We all face different ups and downs in life, including personal trauma, such as illness, loss of a loved one, breakdown of relationships, challenging financial situations, abuse, bullying and other societal challenges that life throws at us.

We may even have shared experiences such as wars, terrorist incidents, natural disasters, and the Queen's passing. It would be remiss of me not to mention the pandemic, the most significant global health crisis of our generation. We must figure our way through and deal with some of life's most challenging paths.

Psychologists say those who can keep calm when dealing with the disasters life throws at us creates resilience. Resilient people can use their skills to deal with challenges rather than keep using coping skills that may not support our well-being in a positive light.

I also believe that we can have different types of resilience depending on what it is and who is involved. It is also worth noting that the person may still feel those emotions; they just deal with them differently.

My own experience of 'resilience' was tested recently. I went through a separation and divorce that was not what I expected at 50—trying to protect our son and challenging myself to think about my actions and their impact on those around us.

Taking control and dealing with different obstacles such as selling homes, buying new ones, dealing with legal issues, and trying to maintain a 'friendly' relationship with my x-partner at times were challenging – and yes, I had days I wanted to scream and shout. Days that I just cried. Days that I said why me. And I bet you can pick and shift this situation to many more in life.

However, I had a belief that things would get better and easier, and they did; not being afraid to cry – is so good that it lets out the anxiety and grief we feel. Making a concerted effort to look after myself, even the basics like eating healthier, exercising, and drinking the correct fluid.

I also decided to limit alcohol intake; when things seem rubbish, you don't need anything else making you feel worse. These are not easy paths to walk, but surrounding yourself with the proper guidance, advice, and love can make the journey a little less lonely.

There are many different types of resilience:

Physical Resilience – this could be how the body recovers from illness or injury.

Mental Resilience – this may be the ability to adapt to changing situations.

Emotional Resilience – regulating emotions in stressful situations.

Social Resilience involves groups or communities bonding together to deal with difficult situations.

Many reports have suggested that people are less resilient when facing events such as the death of a partner, unemployment, and even significant societal events like the pandemic, alone. We all need support from time to time, and part of being resilient is knowing when to ask for help.

Reflection: How many times have you heard bad news and wanted to run for the hills or hide from the world? Resilient people think differently, meet the challenges head-on, plan to deal with what's in front of them, believe it is possible, are flexible and adaptable to their thinking, and take good care of themselves

Activity 1

Stay connected. Build a network of supporters. Your people, those who are honest, provide you with support and guidance and accept you in good and bad times. Write their names down and why they're your people. Use the note pages at the end of this chapter.

Example

Name	Why
Sharron Butterworth	No matter what - Sharron is somebody I can rely on, she loves me unconditionally. Would drop anything to be with me in the bad times and is there to champion me in the good. She is honest, does not always agree with me and is somebody I can trust.
Gill Bryant	Very honest - gives great guidance but also tells me if I am an ass! Huge support in work life gives guidance and advice when required. But does not judge.

NOTE: Create a list, don't be surprised if your circle is small; it's not a numbers game. It is about quality.

Activity 2

Start your day well. Look in the mirror, like what you see and say three things you are grateful for that day. Write them down, if this helps.

Example:

Gratitude 1. I am grateful for Sam, my son, he brings a special light to my life each day.

Gratitude 2. I am grateful for Claire – and although she is no longer here, she has left me with people who support me each day.

Gratitude 3. I am grateful for my home, my sanctuary.

Activity 3

When the bad times arrive – keep telling yourself this is just a moment in time. You will get through this, things will change. Give yourself hope.

Notes

Notes

Notes

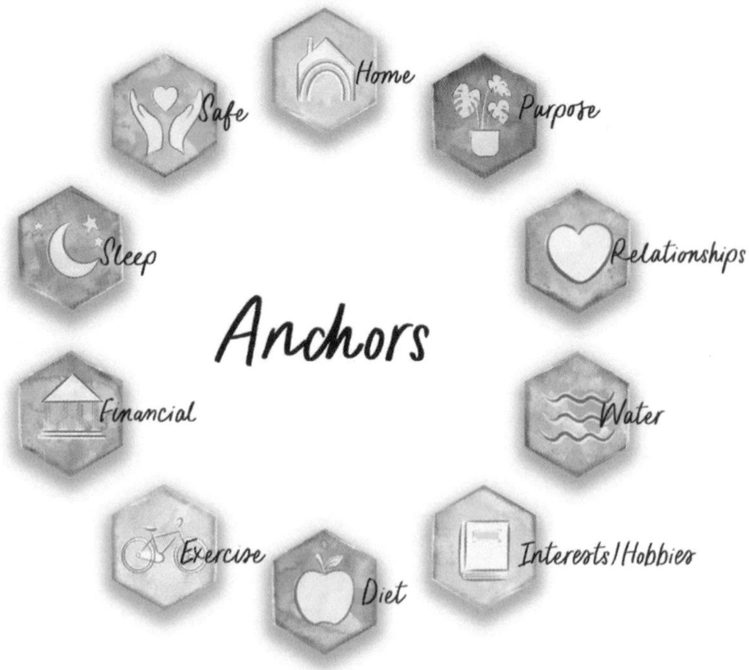
Home
Safe
Purpose
Sleep
Relationships
Anchors
Financial
Water
Exercise
Diet
Interests/Hobbies

7

Anchors

What are my anchors?

'When it rains, look for rainbows.'
Oscar Wilde

Anchors are 'headers' in our lives that we all have; they can keep us on track, and help us to feel safe, wanted and loved. However, we all have different things that take place in our worlds that connect to the different anchors.

We all have things in our world that give us stability. Over the next few pages, we are going to take a look at some standard anchors. Remember that as wonderful, unique individuals, you will have some additional ones that make you, you!

Finance

When we can pay our bills, mortgages, rent, feed our families, and keep them warm, it gives us contentment like no other.

Reflection: Think about a time when this may have been a challenge for you – what impact did it have regarding any worries or concerns?

When you have concerns about finance, it can affect many areas of your life. Can you recall those concerns?

Write them down or reflect.

Common signs are that it can disturb sleep patterns, or it might impact on relationships, or cause our minds to be really busy where we cannot think of anything else.

Think about those in your world who may worry about their jobs or job security. Those who may be struggling with rising costs in the world. Those who have to choose to feed the family or stay warm. You certainly can imagine the desperation.

Home

Our homes can be our place of safety and security. That place where we can kick off our shoes and be ourselves without having to step it up to the outside world.

Reflection: What if our homes are not a safe place to be? A place where we don't want to be.

We know that for some people, domestic abuse and conflict can make home life challenging and, at times, unbearable.

What does your home mean to you? Is it your happy place? Is it a place of safety and security?

Can you recall any concerns when it hasn't been? Why? Write them down or reflect – did it impact any of your other anchors?

NOTE: Please don't feel you have to write something – if your home has been that 'happy' place reverse the question. Write down the positive impact this has on your life.

Relationships

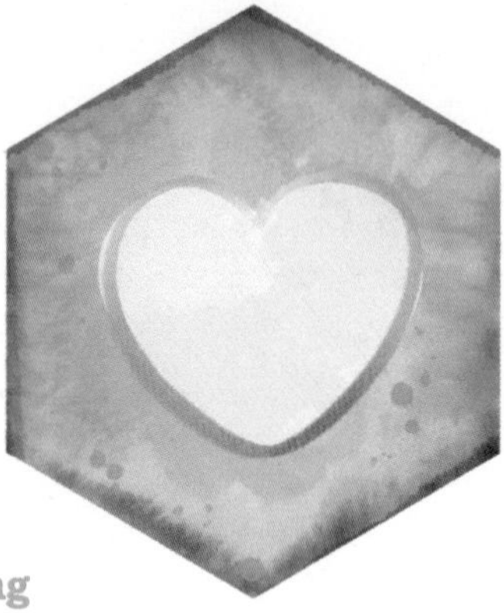

We are human beings, and relationships are important to us. Partners, friends, and work colleagues, all add something to our worlds.

Reflection: What happens when relationships are going through a turbulent time? It might be conflict in the workplace, disagreements with friends or family or even those closer relationships with partners causing you to have a difficult time. I am sure you will agree that these can all equally cause us emotional pain, worry and even concern.

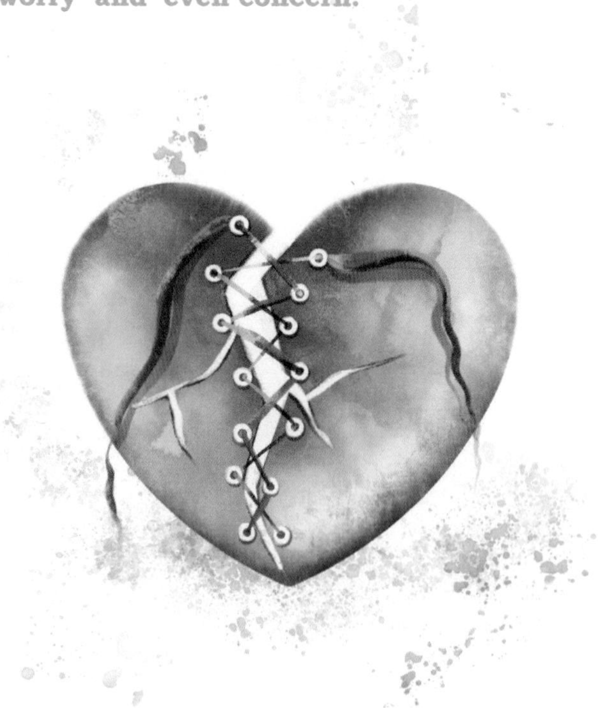

Relationships can be a tricky part of life, and we can all have times of conflict. Write down how this made you feel. Did it impact on any of your anchors?

Hobbies/Interests

These are important because they help us take ourselves into another world, one where we can stop thinking about all that everyday 'stuff'. They can help us feel quite good about ourselves, smile and enjoy.

Reflection: H ow m any p eople d o you know at the start of lockdown, pressed pause and started to do something more creative; cooking, baking, or even being more 'arty'? Sometimes as adults, we forget how important this is to ourselves and how good it makes us feel.

What do you enjoy doing? What helps to make you, you? Write down all your hobbies and interests that take you to that happy place. Also write down how often you get to do them and how they make you feel.

Example:

HOBBIES...	How often do you get to do them and how do they make you feel?
WALKING	EVERY DAY AND AIM FOR 10,000 STEPS (WHICH I DO MOST DAYS). Walking gives me that time out after a busy day and makes me feel more relaxed.
READING	LOVE TO READ. Reality is this is something that I only do on holidays.

Purpose

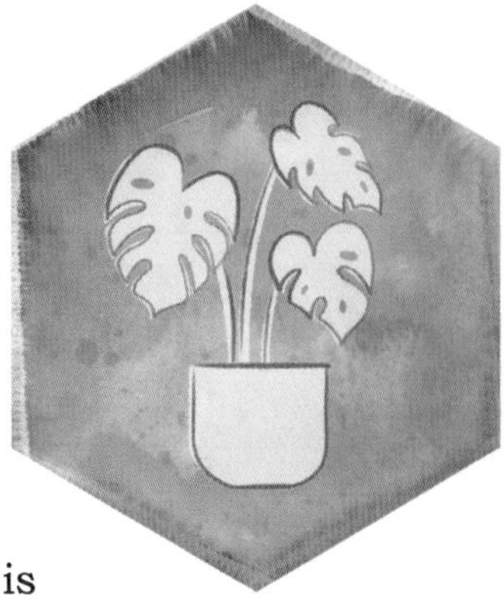

What is the reason you get out of bed for? What is your purpose or even 'purposes?' As adults, we need to have our purpose – it makes us part of our identity. Having a purpose helps us disguise what is important and what is not important. It also gives us clear goals to help us achieve our purpose with direction and meaning.

Reflection: What if you lose your purpose? The role that you have played for a long time. How would you feel about losing the job that has been a big part of you? Feeling a lack of purpose can impact all areas of our life and even contribute to anxiety or depression.

What is your purpose? Write down your purpose and why, and** also **the feeling?

Example:

Purpose	Why	Feeling
Work	I enjoy the work I do supporting people finding solutions and it provides me with fulfilment and fun.	Work helps me to feel like I contribute and that I belong somewhere.

Diet

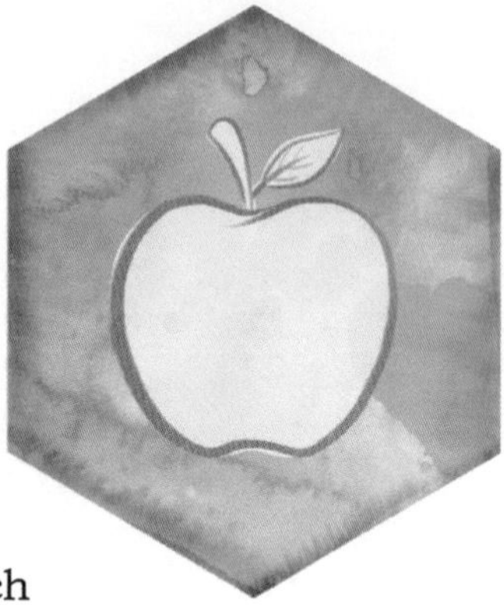

Putting the right foods in our bodies is essential for our overall health; current guidance states five portions of different fruit and vegetables (80g per portion size) daily. However, it can be challenging and confusing for many to watch their sugar and salt intake and not eat carbs.

Below is the World Health Organisation's current guidance.

For adults

A healthy diet includes the following:

- Fruit, vegetables, legumes (e.g., lentils and beans), nuts and whole grains (e.g., unprocessed maise, millet, oats, wheat and brown rice).
- At least 400 g (i.e., five portions) of fruit and vegetables per day, excluding potatoes, sweet potatoes, cassava and other starchy roots.
- Less than 10% of total energy intake from free sugars, which is equivalent to 50g (or about 12 level teaspoons) for a person of healthy body weight consuming approximately 2000 calories per day, but ideally is less than 5% of total energy intake for additional health benefits. Free sugars are all sugars added to foods or drinks by the manufacturer, cook or consumer, and sugars naturally present in honey, syrups, fruit juices, and fruit juice concentrates.
- Less than 30% of total energy intake is from fats. Unsaturated fats (found in fish, avocado and nuts, and in sunflower, soybean, canola and olive oils) are preferable to saturated fats (found in fatty meat,

butter, palm and coconut oil, cream, cheese, ghee and lard) and trans-fats of all kinds, including both industrially-produced trans-fats (found in baked and fried foods, and pre-packaged snacks and foods, such as frozen pizza, pies, cookies, biscuits, wafers, and cooking oils and spreads) and ruminant *trans-fats* (found in meat and dairy foods from ruminant animals, such as cows, sheep, goats and camels). It is suggested that the intake of saturated fats be reduced to less than 10% of total energy intake and *trans-fats* to less than 1% of total energy intake. In particular, industrially produced *trans-fats* are not part of a healthy diet and should be avoided.

- Less than 5g of salt (equivalent to about one teaspoon) per day. Salt should be iodised.

Reflection: Think about our body as that big machine that has to be fuelled correctly. If, as a machine, we don't put the right fuel or amount of fuel in them, then we expect it to splutter and stall. We forget that our body needs care, attention, and love, including the right ingredients to help it perform at the best it can be.

Do you always think about what your body needs?

This is the World Health Organisation's viewpoint on diet:

A healthy diet is essential for good health and nutrition. *It protects you against many chronic non-communicable diseases, such as heart disease, diabetes, and cancer. Eating a variety of foods and consuming less salt, sugars and saturated and industrially produced trans-fats, are essential for a healthy diet.*

Diet can be very contentious for many people, and I know there will be people out there who need extra care, love and support.

I have had to re-educate myself around food and it has been a battle for decades. However, I have started to do a few things differently.

1. *Understand what I am putting into my body each day.*
2. *Am I getting enough fresh fruit and vegetables?*
3. *Cutting back on salt and sugar.*
4. *Eating more fish.*
5. *Being aware that some drinks are not calorie free!*

Think about these questions as a starter.

I have noticed that when I fuel my body in the right way, I am more energised, I sleep better and my skin glows.

Please see the contact page at the end of this journal for those who would like more information or support.

By the way, that is not to say we cannot have some treats; it's about having a balance!

Water/fluid

Water is good for our bodies! We need about two litres a day, and the good news is that it is cheap and calorie-free. If you want to jazz it up, try no-added sugar squash. Fruit tea and caffeine-free coffee/tea can also be better choices.

Reflection: Do you keep yourself hydrated throughout the day? Remember, too much caffeine can impact our anxiety levels; these might also come in the guise of energy drinks, fizzy pop, and traditional drinks like coffee and tea. Try a challenge for 48 hours of cutting out the caffeine – how does your body react?

Take the challenge if you are a caffeine lover. How did it make you feel?

Try a 2lt-2.5lt challenge for 7 days. Did you notice anything about your energy levels? Did you sleep better?

Exercise

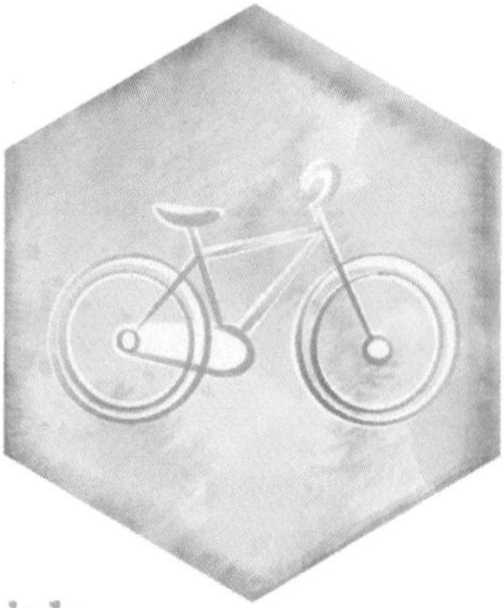

Exercise is good to help with anxiety that builds up in our bodies. About two hours a week or 20 mins a day, to where your heart rate is elevated. It's also a great way to give us timeout and headspace to think.

Reflection: People can be put off by exercise because they think it's about going to the gym and that in itself can be overwhelming. Not having the right gear or body image, and some don't like to exercise in front of others.

Exercise needs to be something you feel you can do and can even change your mindset – this is something that I need to keep myself physically and mentally fit. Small challenges, like going for a 20-minute

walk, can be equally as good. The crux of the matter is finding something you enjoy – even if it's dancing around your kitchen. Or an online activity.

1. How does it make you feel after your exercise?

2. How often is exercise part of your life?

3. Have you thought about trying something new? If so, what? Write down a few ideas.

NOTE: Exercise can mean different things to different people; it is not always about getting sweaty in a gym.

Safe

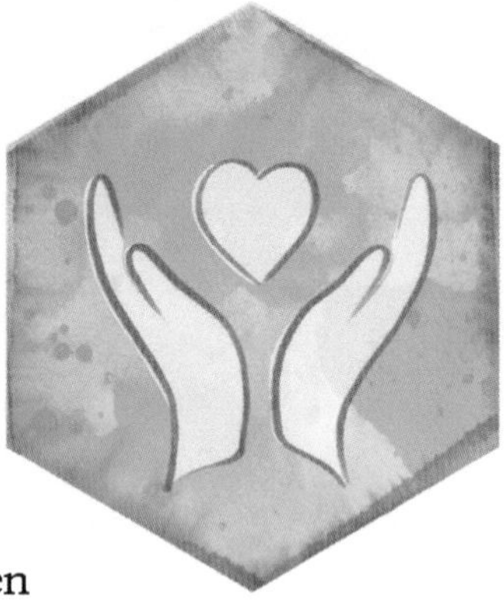

We all like to feel safe, whether in our homes, communities, or workplaces. Many of us take this for granted and view this as being a bit of a given.

For some people pressing pause, understanding when we are feeling different about the situation, and putting in smaller goals to return to normal with a little bit of security, helps us to feel differently about a situation. At times our minds can race, and we also have to be realistic about what we do have control of.

It might even be those news headlines that make us feel negative about our safety, and world events that are taking place can also have an impact.

Reflection: Many things can impact on how we feel safe – the pandemic has led to many people feeling more anxious as we return to those 'normal' things in life. It could be larger gatherings, travelling on public transport or even going on holiday. We have all been told for a few years that it's not safe, so how can we trust now that everything is now ok? How do we get the confidence to start living a normal life?

1. *Reflect on the last few years – has this impacted you or someone you know?*

2. *What 'normal behaviours' have changed?*

3. *Has this impacted on other areas of life?*

Sleep

National Sleep Foundation guidelines advise that healthy adults need between 7 and 9 hours of sleep per night. Babies, young children, and teens need even more sleep to enable their growth and development. People over 65 should also get 7 to 8 hours per night.

What do the statistics say?

- 62% of adults worldwide say they don't sleep as well as they'd like (Philips Global Sleep Survey, 2019).
- As many as 67% of adults report sleep disturbances at least once every night (Philips Global Sleep Survey, 2019).
- 8 in 10 adults worldwide want to improve their sleep, but 60% have not sought help from a medical professional (Philips Global Sleep Survey, 2019).
- 44% of adults worldwide say that sleep quality has worsened over the past five years (Philips Global Sleep Survey, 2019).

Sleep is an essential function that allows your body and mind to recharge, leaving you refreshed and alert when you wake up. Healthy sleep also helps the body remain healthy and stave off diseases. Without enough sleep, the brain cannot function properly.

I go through different sleep patterns, from getting lots of good sleep to having those moments where I wake up at a ridiculous hour and then want to sleep when it is time to get up. Feedback from those around me tells me when I have not had enough sleep! There is nothing like the nearest and dearest to share that is there? But I know

I can be grumpy; things take longer to do, especially my decision-making.

If I am honest, that feeling of exhaustion is like no other. But like most of us, we put on a few invisible cloaks to hide how we are feeling. But it takes a lot of energy, and at a time, I am already feeling empty.

I know what I need to do to even get the basics right, like exercise, eating well, and drinking more water (anyone who knows me knows I am shocking at this, and I have to really manage this one). I also know if there is a specific reason I am waking up. Those life concerns that nip you in the early hours.

How do I cope? I am planning and writing down these frustrations to help me figure out a route to get past them. I am speaking to friends to find a solution. I know that seems easier said than done. But it also gives me those realisation moments when I am trying to control the world, which is impossible. Now I also understand that, at times, these may be challenges with our loved ones; it could be relationships, children, and so many other things that life throws at us.

Looking after 'self' and being self-aware will not stop those life problems from overspilling onto us. However, give yourself the best chance to cope by knowing 'you' and loving 'you', assessing your anchors and knowing when behaviours may change.

We need to remind ourselves that we are all unique, loved and very special people and treat ourselves with the same love and respect we give others. If only to survive.

Reflection:

- Are you productive, healthy, and happy on seven hours of sleep? Or have you noticed that you require more hours of sleep to get into high gear?
- Do you have co-existing health issues? Are you at higher risk for any disease?
- Do you have a high level of daily energy expenditure? Do you frequently play sports or work in a labour-intensive job?
- Do your daily activities require alertness to do them safely? Do you drive every day and/or operate heavy machinery? Do you ever feel sleepy when doing these activities?
- Are you experiencing, or do you have a history of, sleeping problems?
- Do you depend on caffeine to get you through the day?
- When you have an open schedule, do you sleep more than you do on a typical workday?

1. *How is your sleep?*

2. *Is there anything keeping you awake at night?*

3. *Do you have a nightly routine to wind down?*

4. *What can you do to ensure a better night's sleep?*

Notes

Notes

Notes

Notes

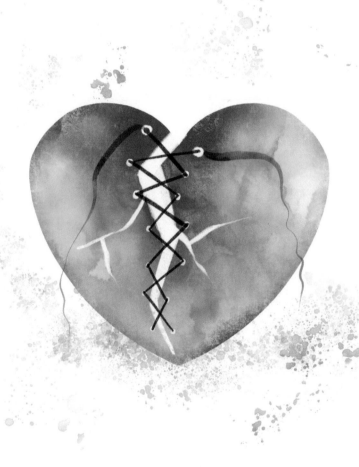

8

Life's Curve Balls!

Curve Balls

So, what is a curve ball? My view on a curve ball is something that you don't expect – at times, this may be a good thing, it is not always bad.

Imagine you are walking down your road of life. Let's focus on your career – you know what your dream is, you know where you are going and then 'bang', four different roads appear in front of you. Now you are in a quandary – which road is the right road? All may have opportunities, but which one is for you? What if I take the wrong road? What will happen? What if I make a mess? Will I look silly?

We can see how those doubts might start to build some anxiety into our worlds. An added layer to this is that something else may take place too – it might be the death of a loved one – again unexpected, and even if expected, it can still leave a deep despair of shock. For some people, it may be that their worlds have just been flooded with emotions, hurt, loss, and loneliness. Be mindful, though, that we all are unique and deal with things differently.

Grief

I think we have all experienced a loss of some sort in our lives. My earliest impact of grief was when I was fifteen and my grandma passed away. I can still distinctly remember that knock on the door when my grandad and Uncle came to give the news to my mum. She screamed, and the full impact of grief hit her body like a ton of bricks.

For me, it was jointly the pain of the love of a significant role model and the overwhelming feeling of emptiness, along with my mum in so much pain.

Visibly it was hard to watch. Over the years, many of us will feel that pain. Losing a loved one is an obvious sign of grief and the pain that accompanies it. We also feel the loss of many other things in our world: lost jobs, the end of relationships, change, loss of our freedoms and loss of anything familiar.

The pandemic highlighted that last one to many of us so dramatically, and so significantly, that it will impact us for many years to come. However, we may not recognise this as grief.

We all have a view and judgement on how people should react or behave, but we must remember that grief is unique to everyone. When I recall my first loss – I can remember thinking I didn't know how to deal with this loss, and it was hard to navigate. There is a grief cycle that many of us will go through; below are the eight stages.

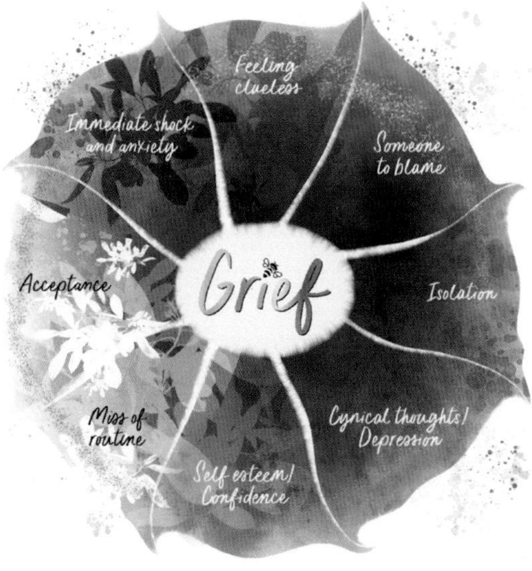

Grief
Feeling clueless
Someone to blame
Isolation
Cynical thoughts/ Depression
Self esteem/ Confidence
Miss of routine
Acceptance
Immediate shock and anxiety

So, let's take the grief of losing a job.

1. Immediate shock – 'me, it's really me on the list of people losing their job – nooooooooooo!!! How will I pay the bills?' The brain goes straight into overdrive.
2. Feeling clueless – 'I so didn't see that coming. I am brilliant at what I do – why me?'
3. Someone to blame – 'well, it's because my manager has never liked me – I am just not a 'yes' person.'
4. Isolation – 'Then fine, I am just going to give the basics – I am not getting involved. If they don't want me, they can't have me!'
5. Cynical thoughts/depression – 'It's because I am rubbish – who would blame them.'
6. Self-esteem and confidence – 'I don't have the energy. I am not going to find something else.' Little voices going into overdrive.
7. Miss of routine – 'miss the place, grabbing a coffee, chatting to everyone, having a giggle. I even miss the journey!'
8. Acceptance – 'Ok, let's create a plan. I need to find something else!'

Reflection – think about a situation when you have felt grief – do you recognise any of these behaviours?

What we do need to be mindful of is that some people get stuck in 4,5 & 6. That's when we might need to think about how we can support that person and direct them to support.

What do you recognise in yourself when you have experienced grief – circle the numbers that resonate with how you feel right now.

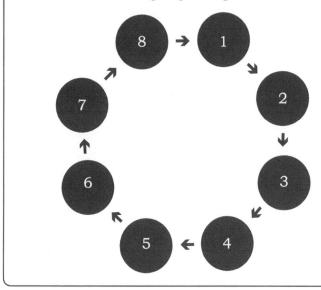

This section about grief is dedicated in memory of Claire, my oldest dear friend, taken from us way too soon but never forgotten.

Further Reflections:

- Write down each week/month everything that is going on in your world.
- Hold on to those good memories – they help.
- Don't be afraid to talk to other people about their grief - this helps release those thoughts and feelings.
- One of the most thoughtful things for me was a friend turning up with a garden plant – to nurture and grow so I can continually remember and share those happy times.

Reflect on the numbers circled in the diagram and write down what you can do that will help.

Isolation

Some of the biggest challenges even before the pandemic were isolation and loneliness. The following phrase has stayed with me for many years.

I can still feel lonely – even when I am in a room with a thousand people.

A phrase that I understand entirely. When I was going through my separation, I felt an overwhelming fear of being on my own and not knowing where to go or what decisions to make. Not particularly about day-to-day decisions at work or in my new home, but a stillness that if I stopped completely, everything would fall apart. I can remember feeling everything was changing, and that I had no control.

There were many days when I just cried. I suppose that was also a fear of my future. What would life be like? Certainly not what is happening here and now. I can never forget a close friend asking if I was okay. I gave the standard answer, and she replied, 'you are running this like an HR project plan – are you sure?'

At that point, I was probably 60-40 – the latter being that emptiness. But taking control helped me to feel better. Everybody's journey is different, and we have to acknowledge it.

Reflection:

- **Emotions are good – let yourself cry if that is what you want to do.**
- **Tell yourself this is a normal reaction, especially when you feel that frustration.**
- **This is truly just a moment in time, and it will get better.**
- **Look at your champions around you – talk to them about how you feel. I am very fortunate to have a number of them - Sharron, Anna, Julie, Alisa, Kerry, Gill, Richard, David – my army.**
- **Aim for small goals; these goals help you get there with baby steps!**

What small goals – can you take?

Goal 1

Goal 2

Goal 3

Note: Try not to run too far ahead, small steps are important to your journey.

Notes

Notes

Notes

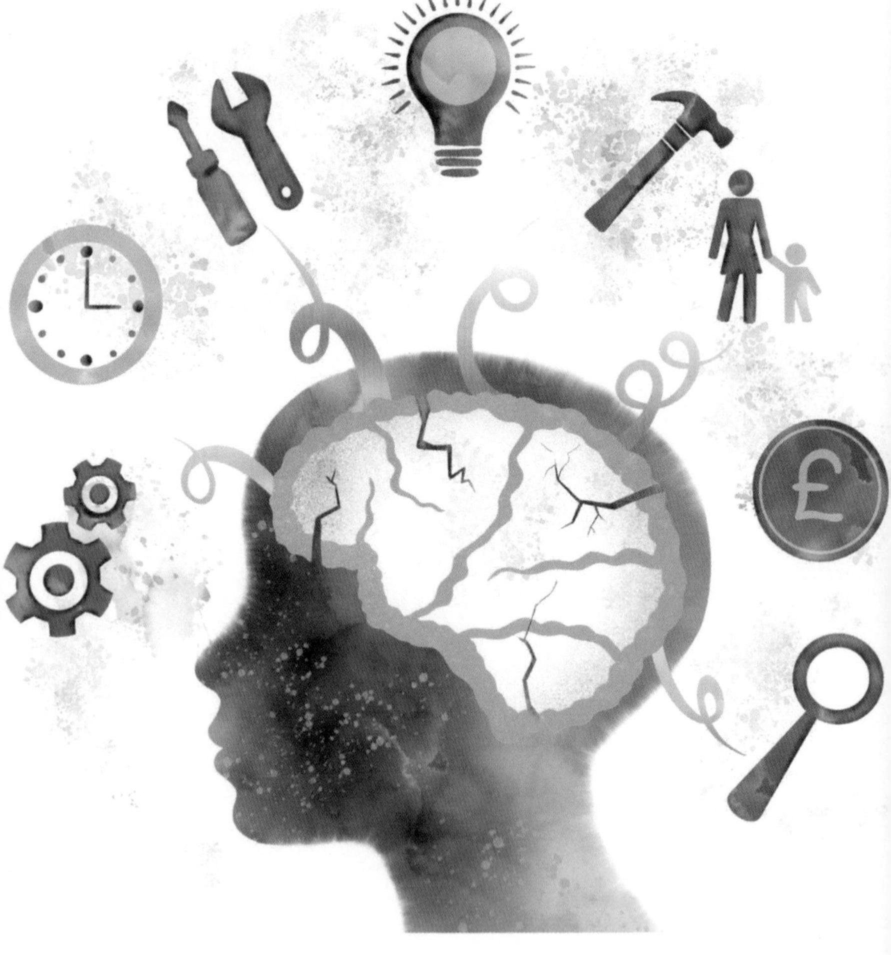
£

9

Work In Progress

I am a work in progress.

As human beings, we have very high expectations of ourselves, but we do not necessarily make sure that our bodies are match fit for the journey of life. Selfcare is a priority and our responsibility.

Question? When you look in the mirror, do you like what you see? Do you love yourself? Do you believe you are deserving? I believe you are – every single one of you.

This book allows you to put yourself front, centre and back. Journal your journey.

Reflection:

- **Write down what you want out of life.**
- **Plan what you need to get on the journey towards your goal.**
- **What can pull you away from your journey?**
- **Who can support you?**
- **Build yourself up each day and silence those critical voices.**
- **Talk.**

Write your plan. Start with immediate goals, medium and long term. Review them and change them if your focus changes.

Life Goal

Life Goal

Life Goal

Life Goal

Life Goal

Life Goal

Notes

Notes

Notes

Notes

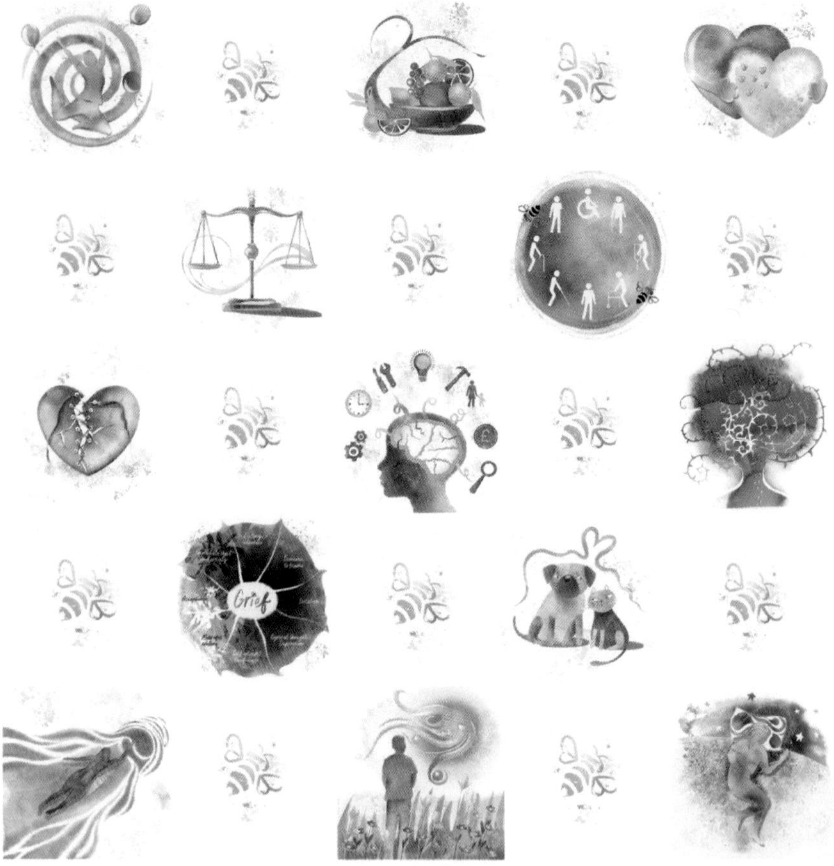
Grief

10

Further Reflections

We all must remember that life is not perfect. We are all going to have ups and downs. We have information constantly coming at us, communication that does not stop. It can be exhausting; this book is designed to give you guidance, not to lecture you, but to help you press that pause button and think about yourself—the wonderful unique you. I have taken my own experience, challenges, and personal joys to help you on your own journey. Things that have worked for me both past and present.

The one thing I have not covered is pets and how much these wonderful fur balls of fun can help with many of your life anchors. I have two Labradoodles, Barnaby and Leo, whom I co-parent (yes, we are a modern-day family). They have helped me in times of loneliness, made me laugh, and made me go out and get exercise (ugghhh – yes, I have felt that uggh on some days). They give me so much love; at times, they have given me purpose and, of course, a big fluffy cuddle.

When you reflect on this journal, use it as a unique tool for your thoughts and feelings. Don't just concentrate on 'stuff' going wrong or overwhelming you; think of all that is good in your world. And remember to hold on to that 'hope', the hope that things can change. Learn and understand more about you, which will continue to build your resilience.

Reference

https://www.verywellmind.com/what-is-resilience-2795059

https://www.who.int/news-room/fact-sheets/detail/healthy-diet

https://www.sleepfoundation.org/how-sleep-works/how-much-sleep-do-we-really-need

https://www.singlecare.com/blog/news/sleep-statistics/

https://www.who.int/initiatives/behealthy/healthy-diet

https://mhfaengland.org

(All links current at time of going to press).

Contact me ...

Email: info@uknphc.com

Website:
https://wellness-journal.co.uk/

Instagram:
https://www.instagram.com/thewellnessjournalexpert/

Facebook:
https://www.facebook.com/wellnessjournalexpert

LinkedIn: Sharon (Pegg) Kinder FCIPD

THANK YOU'S

You can never write something like this without saying a huge thank you to so many people in my life: my role models, my saviours, my icons, my friends – MY PEOPLE.

Sam – you are simply the best thing in my life. Thank you for your love and your friendship. You make me proud to be your mum every day.

My mum – the woman who totally believes in everything I do. Wiped my tears and gave loving support at every step. She really is an icon! Love you, Mum.

Sharron – My sister from another mother, my soul mate, my BF. Always there thick and thin, this journey of life its highs and lows, and I am so grateful that you are travelling it with me.

Kerry – We have such a solid friendship, another anchor in my life – love ya, babe.

Gill- We have known each other for years and years – you are basically me and I you! Thank God I have a travel buddy to go with to the leadership conferences.

Richard M – Wow, meeting you was like a light coming into my world! David – I will be and always will your Lady 300. Posh Brummie – Words cannot describe our friendship, and I feel a simple thank you is not enough, but I know you understand what I mean.

Amanda, my work supporter, you're amazing.

Perrin – my matchmaker on the social scene, my friend, my mischief partner. This book would not have happened if it wasn't for you and the introduction to Gail.

Gail, your expertise, guidance, and motivation have kept me going.

Ivy, a huge thank you for taking it out of my head and being able to create the most beautiful illustrations. Your talent takes my breath away.

THANK YOU, XXX

Notes

Notes

Notes

Notes

Notes

_____

_____

_____

_____

_____

_____

_____

_____

_____

_____

_____

_____

_____

_____

_____

_____

_____

Notes

Notes

Notes

Notes

Notes

Notes